Romantic Moments

Poetry for Couples in Love

Larry Roop

Imagine Poetry

ISBN: 978-1-7333212-0-4

Front cover image by Photographer Mohamed Thasneem
Book layout by Oprahgraphic

First Printing Edition 2019

Imagine Poetry
75 Reba Ave
Mansfield, Ohio 44907

www.imaginepoetry.com

Dedication

Foremost to my dear and loving wife Amy, thank you for many years of sharing your love, passion, devotion and commitment to always keeping our marriage strong.

And to strong loving couples everywhere.

Epigraph

"Can anything else hold such intensity and fire,
Igniting the fuse to our deepest desires?"

Table of Contents

Introduction

For those that like their poetry in what is sometimes call traditional rhyming style, then this book is for you. There is one poem that lends itself to free verse. Also, we have you covered on some of the best modern romantic poems as well.

If your love runs deep with the one you are with and you experience depth and passion almost always you will find that this book of romantic poems will have you wanting more as you read each line.

Are My Words Enough

When words are all I have
To express how I feel
Are words enough to help you,
Understand my love is real?

The distance that lies between us
Are really miles apart
Are words enough to tell you
How I feel within my heart?

Are the simple lines I say to you
Enough to hold your thoughts
To center them around me,
No matter what the cost?

Do you feel the understanding
In the words I have to say
Does the romantic words I write
Stay with you throughout the day?

Do certain words make you smile
And brighten up the times
That always seem to get you down
When you're lost within your mind?

We can't always be together
So for now these words I share
To help you understand my love
How much I truly care.

As Close As We Can Be

I hold out my hand, you place it in yours
You whisper so gentle, such sweet soft words
You run your delicate fingers, through my dark hair
I feel your deep love within the night air.

I hold your soft body, I stare into your eyes,
The beauty within you, is in the night skies,
And I know right now, as you are here with me
We are as close as ever we will be.

Never more than right now, so deep within my soul
Do I feel the love you give, so strong and in control
The passion that's rising, the flames in the night,
That one burning desire, as I hold you so tight.

Where does this end? Will we always be together?
will the thoughts of our minds, travel this road forever?
It's hard to really say, since the future we can't see,
But we are as close, as ever we will be.

For now my darling angel let the night take us away
To another world, another place where we can love and play,
And let this be the moment, that stays within our minds,
Holding onto the memories that are with us throughout time.

Darling It's Good to Know

Darling it is good to know
That you're a part of my life,
That you can brighten up my world
Through heartache, grief and strife.

Because you always know the words
That help me through each day,
That I can count you being there
Along each step of the way.

How much does that mean to me?
More than you will know
For sometimes it's the simple things
That you only need to show.

For my heart can usually tell
When a certain love is there,
When feelings go beyond the walls
Of how much you really care.

So it's important that you know
Life's treasure is not always gold
But just to feel your special love
And having you to hold.

Desires of the Heart

I enter our room and walk to your side
You stand there so lovely, like a wedding day bride.
Your beautiful soft hair glows from the light
Of all the candles lit, on this romantic night.

To me you're a lady of such beauty and charm
Your smile is enchanting, as you come to my arms.
And as I hold you tight, never wanting to let go,
The passion is rising, and your eyes are aglow.

So my precious angel, let me take you away
To only those places where lovers can play
To show you my love, that burning desire
That only your heart longs to acquire.

And for all that I hold, and with all that I give,
I'll make this night special as long as you live.
And take you to places you dreamed in your mind
Would last for eternity through the fabric of time.

Do You Feel This Moment?

As you look so deep
Into the sunset skies
Do you see the same beauty
That I see in your eyes?

Do you feel my gentle touches
Going through your soft hair?
Do you feel the warm breeze
Flowing through the night air?

Do you believe that this moment
Is truly meant to be
And that all feels so right,
As you're standing here with me?

For now, I truly know,
Your're my very special girl,
With a love in your heart
That brightens up my world.

So may I just say,
As we stand here together,
I want you always in my life
So I can hold you forever.

Dream

Dream of magic moments
that often will come true
Dream of sunset beaches
On them, me and you.

Dream of romantic dinners
Sipping wine by the fire
Dream of making love
Beyond your heart's desire.

Dream of slow massages
As my hands rub your skin.
Dream of passionate kisses,
As I hold you close within.

Dream forever in this moment
That will last throughout time
Dream you will always love me
Forever in your mind.

Dream so many dreams
That they fill your mind with love,
For in the dreams I have at night
It is you, I dream of.

Even in the Rain

My love, I don't want to miss a moment
Of having you here beside me.
Even as the rain pours down around us,
Your love keeps me warm.

I never thought or even knew,
Just a few years ago,
That I would have someone so beautiful,
So perfect to love me for who I am.

And still further, I would have never known
Every feeling, every thought you give me now
Could touch my heart, mind, and soul
Affecting emotions I did not know existed.

My precious angel even in this pouring rain
I know how wonderful and special you are.
And sometimes I may feel like I do not deserve
To have you as my best friend and my lover.

But know forever I will always try
Too please, honor, and cherish you.
Be a man you can feel proud to know
And hold so deeply within your heart.

I Never Wanted More

Hold me, darling, forever
As we look at the sunset sky.
Let me feel you warm and tender
As I gaze into your eyes.

Let this wonderful moment last
Long into the night,
As I kiss your lips so passionately,
As the moon shines its light.

For my darling angel,
I never wanted more
Than to be here with you
Along this golden shore.

And being with you now
Has made a dream come true,
Lost in your radiant beauty
That could only come from you.

And even though the years from now
Will someday fade away,
I know my mind will drift again
Back to this perfect day.

I Want to Be the One

I want to be the one, my love
That lifts you above the clouds,
Opening up your longing spirit
To all that we're allowed.

I want to make you feel alive
To reach out and take a chance,
Explore new places never lived before,
To dance like you've never danced.

Give me your hand and your heart
And all that I acquire
To open up a wonderful world
That will set your soul on fire.

Let me show you all the future holds,
The life that could exist
Within the realms of love's desire
And the passion within the kiss.

For every day I will give to you
New thoughts to fill your mind
So come with me, and be set free
To all that we shall find.

Imagine

Imagine the two of us
Somewhere far away
Feeling the warmth of the sun,
Sharing the beauty of the day.

Imagine us walking,
Holding each other tight
As God paints a sunset
On an evening sky so bright.

Imagine us looking deep
Into each other's eyes,
Remembering times of happiness
Or the tears that we have cried.

Its hard to say in words
What all you mean to me,
But imagine forever, my love
You're where I want to be.

For each day I share with you
Is one more day together
That I can hold you close to me
And love you, darling, forever.

In the Heart of the Kiss

In the heart of the kiss, the passion arises;
The body gives way to all new surprises.
The look in her eyes cuts through to his soul
The restraint for this moment now loses control.

The fervent heat that two bodies possess,
Longing for release, within their caress
The movement of his fingers, in places long touched
Confirms his desire to love her so much.

He picks her up, and lays her down,
Thoughts of the moment forever abounds.
She holds on tightly to all that is given
On a night so sensual and passion-driven.

Upward and forward the night rages on,
As a couple on fire, makes love till dawn.
And so it goes, may you never forget
What passion might come from the heart of the kiss.

It's All Part of Love

The flowers that bloom
in the springtime air,
The laughter of children
that you hear everywhere,

The morning dew
That kisses the ground
It is all part of love,
Where love is found.

The summer sun
That heats up the day,
The way you look,
The words you say.

The rainbow in the sky
That comes from above
Is just another example,
It is all part of love.

It's the feelings we feel,
The times that we share
Its knowing forever
You will always be there.

It's the very special moments
That you always dream of,
For you, my wonderful darling,
It is all part of love.

Lost in Beautiful Thought

When you're lost within beautiful thoughts,
Where does your mind go?
Do you hold me deep within your dreams,
Ever knowing I love you so?

Do romantic images fill those times
When you need to feel such love,
Like walking on a sunset beach
Or make love under the stars above?

Do those special pictures take you back
To all we've shared and done?
Do they hold you close and make you feel
That you're my only one?

Tell me my sweet darling,
When you're in your special place
Does your smile put a glow
Upon your beautiful face?

I know my angel, who you are
When I hold you close to me,
But I want to know, when you're alone
Am I all that your mind sees?

Lost Within Your Beauty

Lost within your beauty
Is a great place to be:
A special place that holds,
All the wonder I can see.

A place that truly takes me
Sailing even higher
By the yearning of your body;
That sets my soul on fire.

For it is this burning flame
That draws me close to you
Holding thought to every word
And every dream come true.

And when we're making love
It's our hearts, that set us free
To explore all our passion,
So deep in you and me.

And so my wonderful darling,
Let us hold on to the night,
Fulfilling all we long for
Until the morning brings its light.

Love Whispers

Love whispers ever softly
As you hold me right now,
Deep within your heartbeat
You steal my breath somehow

I feel you so close to me
Your love pulsing through my veins
Breathing new life in me
My heart forever remains.

The warmth that shines in your eyes
Now flows throughout my soul
I feel love's true existence
So strong and in control.

And so you have proven
I need you everyday
To open my longing spirit
In so many beautiful ways.

Love Whispers Softly

Our Special Place

Picture in your mind,
A place we can go,
A place that can hide us
From the world that we know:

A place that can take us,
To lands far beyond,
Where every thought is spoken,
And our love remains strong.

We can hold each other close,
Walk among the trees,
See nature all around us,
As we feel the gentle breeze.

Sit down beside a lake,
As the water reflects the sky
Giving me a chance
To see the beauty in your eyes.

So let me take you now,
To this very special place
Where every magic moment
Puts a smile upon your face,

And to share in our happiness,
Our joy and our fun
Knowing I will be
Forever your special one.

Passion of the Night

The fireplace lit,
The fire all aglow,
Amber flames were flickering
And the music playing low.

A slow playing song,
A bottle of wine,
Sharing the moments
Of your heart and mine.

I slowly kissed you
And held you so tight,
As this moment lingered,
Long into the night.

Then I pulled the strings,
That held your gown in place;
It slid off your tender body,
As a smile came to your face.

You whispered in my ear,
Those sweet sensual words,
"Take me tonight,
For tonight I'm all yours."

And from that moment on,
The passion never died.
Our love grew only stronger,
As you stayed by my side.

Passion's Light

I lay down close beside you;
As I look deep into your eyes,
I feel your tender heartbeat
And hear your whispered sighs.

Your long dark, beautiful hair,
Flowing gently within the wind,
Accents your warm and beautiful face,
As each thought now grows within.

And with each touch of longing desire,
Consuming our very soul
It was not long for destiny's spark
To ignite and take control.

So I held you tight with such embrace,
As if only this moment forever
Would lend our lips to every kiss
And each movement we felt together,

For we set in motion a blazing fire
That burned throughout the night
With fervent heat that forged a love
So strong in passion's light.

Remember When

Remember when, my darling
When we were young and free,
We felt the passion of the night
In who we wanted to be.

We've lived life to the fullest
In everything we've done,
Holding on to each day
With laughter, joy, and fun.

And still with many years gone by
We're a testament to our youth:
I show the world you're still my girl
In a love bound in truth.

For we still hold the magic
And key to our success.
We love each day, finding ways
To relive our happiness.

And what could be greater
Than reliving all those times,
Knowing our future moments
Will bring memories to our minds.

I Love You So Much

Sharing My Life with You

Forever is a long time
To share a special love,
But holding you beside me
Has been all I think of.

For I knew you were special,
Right from the very start
And that you'd always be
Forever in my heart.

For together our lives hold
More than words could ever say,
More than feelings that we felt,
Upon our wedding day.

And through the joy and laughter,
Through all the tears we cried,
All the moments we struggled,
We did it by each other's side.

So my wonderful darling,
As we continue to always be
Close and full of spirit,
New wonders we will see.

And we will share each day
With a renewed love for life,
Doing it always together,
Fulfilled as husband and wife.

Single Rose of Love

Darling I give to you
A single rose of love
Just a little reminder
You're all I'm thinking of.

Such a flower of beauty,
I give to you today
To let you know you're special,
In so many wonderful ways.

For out of all the flowers,
The rose holds the key
To the happiness I give to you,
As you share your world with me.

So darling accept this rose,
May it live long within your heart
And believe our love will strengthen,
Even when we're far apart.

Somewhere Far Away

Let's get lost on a beach
Somewhere far away,
Where we can run, have fun,
Or love throughout the day.

For my darling angel
You deserve something new:
A quiet place to hide away
Where I can be with you.

Nobody to interrupt us,
No phone for miles around,
Just the sound of our hearts
As we watch the sun go down.

And when the morning comes
I can look into your eyes
Remembering the night of passion
Underneath the star lit sky.

Springtime Dream

I gaze upon the flowers
That surround me everywhere,
The gentle breeze that touches me
Reminds me you are there.

I hold you close within my thoughts:
Your reflection looks at me.
I feel as though you're in my soul
No closer could we be.

Oh let the beauty of springtime
Always take us far away,
Where we can be young and free
Forever in this day.

And never lose what we possess
That binds our hearts and minds,
Forever knowing that you, my love,
Will love me throughout time.

The Dream

Last night I had a dream
Of a very beautiful place.
I looked around to find you
And soon felt your strong embrace.

You held me deep in your arms
As if never to let go,
And as your lips were pressed to mine
I knew I loved you so.

For your hunger and your passion
Were fuel for my burning fire.
They ignited the fuse, to my heart
That held my deepest desire.

And I knew no other person
Could affect me the way you do,
Taking control of my body and soul
As I surrendered myself to you.

But then I finally awoke
As the morning showed its light,
Remembering how you held me close
All through the moonlit night.

And even though it was a dream
Reality can still be ours
For someday soon we'll touch for real
And make love beneath the stars.

The Thought of Losing You

I couldn't bear the thought
Of a day without you here,
Your soft gentle spoken words
Or your touches when you are near,

The times you hold me
And tell me I'm the one
Who'll bring you joy and laughter
Through happiness and fun.

The times you just reach out
To have me close to you,
That I may feel your tenderness
In the way that you move.

You know darling you mean so much
That words cannot describe
The many thoughts I have of you
As each passing day goes by.

It would be so very hard
To live one day alone,
To not feel you close to me
Or hear your voice on the phone.

And the thought of losing you
For now, too much to bear,
For my mind would never think
You will ever not be there.

The Way You Make Me Feel

I hold you close beside me,
As your voice comes through the phone
I hold you close beside me
When you sing to me alone.

Every word that you whisper,
Every sigh that you breathe,
Every thought that you're thinking
Holds special meaning just for me.

And the way you say "I love you"
Is more precious than all the gold
Is it truly any wonder
That it's you I want to hold?

Not a day passes by me
That you are not a part
Of all that surrounds me
And lives within my heart.

For you started out a person
Who became my special friend
And feelings grew much deeper
That would last until the end.

It's for all these reasons
And so many, many more
That you will always be a part
Of what I'm longing for.

Thoughts of Love

I spoke to you
One quiet night,
As I felt your love
Surround me tight.

I made each word
Flow in rhyme
As our two hearts
Slowly beat in time.

You whispered gently
Into my ear,
"I feel so at rest
When you are near.

This calm and peace
Holds me tender,
As my body now
To you surrenders.

Come fill me up
With all I need
Allow my spirit,
To be set free.

Let it soar
To heights unknown
As you give your love
To me alone."

To Everything I Dream

When talking to you, darling,
I feel everything is right,
That holding you and loving you
Is all part of my life.

For sweetheart, you may never know
Exactly how I feel,
Exactly how I think of you
In dreams that feel so real.

Mystic lands, enchanted worlds,
Places yet not seen
All hold special thoughts
To everything I dream.

My mind drifts and wanders
Images pass me by:
Passionate tender moments
Together, you and I.

For you see how real it becomes:
When I lay down to sleep
I feel I hold the world
When holding you so deep.

Visions so pure and lovely
Project upon a screen
Visions that hold new meaning
To everything I dream.

To Forever and Always

To forever and always
There will always be
The two of us together,
Forever you and me.

I cannot see the future
Without you always there,
Holding on to past memories
Or times we use to share.

For it's you that makes my life,
My hopes, my dreams so real,
And it's holding you, the way I do,
That is special in how I feel.

And I want you to always know
I'll always be there for you
That you will never face alone
Any problems that you do.

So keep me in your heart
And in your mind with love
Remembering forever and always
It is you I'm dreaming of.

To Have You Here

To have you here,
Me holding you tight,
To be together
Throughout the long night.

To kiss your lips
With passion on fire,
To know you're mine
With such deep desire.

It's been a long time
Since I felt this way,
Enchanted by your touches
And all that you say.

And if this feeling can last,
Then let it go on
You being here now
Is where I belong.

And to always be apart
Of your world full of love
Will be times I hold dear
In all I dream of.

To Love an Angel

I look at you in soft surrender
My arms holding you tight
Your body feels like soothing warmth
As you lay with me tonight.

What have I done my dearest love,
To deserve your heavenly smile?
Am I among the privileged few
To hold an angel for awhile?

Looking deep in your soft warm eyes
Your love surrounds me now
And gives to us passion's fire
As only our souls allow.

So kiss me, darling, make love to me
And be my only desire
For you my love are all I'll need
And all my heart requires.

And if I had just one wish,
It would be our love together.
To hold our hearts and our minds
In this perfect moment forever.

To Love You Forever

If it was my wish my, darling
It would be to love you forever,
To always hold you close to me,
Two lives as one together.

To make you feel so special
Each day in all we've done
To show you always my angel,
That you are my only one.

For you're my inspiration
My hopes and dreams come true,
For everything I long to hold
I only find in you.

You always bring out the best in me
You allow my light to shine,
But brighter still our love remains
In the Architect's grand design.

So thank you always for being there,
No matter where we have gone,
And may the rest of our journey together,
Through our love continue on.

Together at Sunset

The evening sets, the sky all aglow
The colors of sunset beginning to show.
The beauty that lies in the sky so clear:
The way I feel when you are near.

The moments we share hand-in-hand
Feeling the ocean breeze as we walk through the sand.
And soon the sun fades as I look in your eyes,
Our bodies lie down beneath the night skies.

And as we look up into the night,
Your body reaches to hold mind so tight,
Taking me away to a far-off place
Where the desires of the heart, light up your face

And from that moment, love will be made,
Ushering in to a brand new day,
And knowing forever you will always be
That one special person, sharing life with me.

What My Heart Longed to Know

My heart beats in silent thoughts
As I look into your eyes.
I feel the love you give to me
beneath the summer skies.

The love my heart longed to know:
I never thought would come.
Now it fills my every pore
Like the warmth of the noon-day sun.

You fill the void, the emptiness
That stayed within my soul ,
And gave me back what I had lost
So very long ago.

The feelings now, we have shared
Every thought yet unspoken.
I hold them all, within the walls
Of treasured glass unbroken.

For you have restored my faith
In all that I hold true,
So now and forever my love
My heart belongs to you.

When I Hold You

When I hold you close beside me,
I feel your loving touch
I feel the warmth of your body
That says "I love you so very much."

When I wrap you in my arms,
I know you feel secure;
Your smile says "I need you
And I always want you near."

For Darling always know
There will never be a time
That I will ever leave you
Or you won't be on my mind.

For every day I think of you
And hold you close to me.
There's no other place in life
Where I'd would rather be.

So always understand my love
It will always be you
That holds the key to my heart,
As long as I hold you.

When I Look Into Your Eyes

When I look into your eyes,
I see the stars shine at night:
I feel a bit of heaven
As I hold you so tight.

I see the quiet rivers
And the mighty ocean tides;
I feel the love you give to me
When you are by my side.

Then there are the rainbows
Shooting across the sky
Just one of the many wonders
I see within your eyes.

For there are many visions
That you help me to see,
The never ending beauty
That shines in you for me.

And if looking into your eyes
Makes my dreams come true
Let me look at them forever
When I am holding you.

When I Tell You I Love You

When I tell you I love you,
I hope you understand
How much those words truly mean
From the heart of this humble man.

For every moment you're in my life
I feel our love give way
To all the wonders yet unexplored
Fulfilling each passing day.

To hold you close and feel your touch,
To know right from the start
That all your love yet ungiven
Fulfills my longing heart.

That's why I'm blessed every day
To have you in my life
To be the husband I need to be
To have you as my wife.

So my wonderful darling
I hope you always believe
When I tell you that I love you
You're the only one for me.

Your Beauty

Today my darling angel,
I look deep into your eyes
And see the stars of heaven,
As I hold you by my side.

For there could never be one
Who's beauty comes shining through
As much as yours shines for me,
As I make sweet love to you.

For your passion and desire
Reach out to hold me tight,
Taking control of my body and soul
All through the moonlit night.

And no other place would I rather be
Than here, in this moment of time
Lost in your radiant beauty
That forever stays in my mind.

Future Happenings

I want to thank you for purchasing my book, I hope you really enjoyed all the romantic poems dealing with couples in love that I offered you in this selection. In the future you can expect more romantic poetry to come your way.

But to let you know the next book coming out soon will be dealing with spiritual themes. While I do enjoy writing romantic poetry I also love to write about spiritual things as well.

The title of my next book is called Spiritual Awareness Poems about God, His Word, Marriage, and the Nation.

So if you are a Born Again Christian, one who cares about spiritual things in relationship to His Word Marriage and where are nation is heading or you have just became a fan of my poetry and the style in which I write then for sure be on the look out for Spiritual Awareness coming out in the very near future, I am sure you will not be disappointed at all.

For the Farther Future

Books of Poetry dealing with Friendships, Weddings, and even one dealing with The 'Middle Ages' Poems of Castles, Kings, Queens and Knights.

Where to Reach Me

If you have any comments, questions, suggestions or would just like to drop me a line saying thanks. Please do not hesitate to write me at info@imaginepoetry.com please include your e-mail address as well.

In the future we will be having samples of my poetry that we can send out in PDF form to those interested. Send me a note to the above address and let me know you would like a sample and we will put you on the list. Please be sure to include your e-mail address as well.

Printed in Poland
by Amazon Fulfillment
Poland Sp. z o.o., Wrocław